COMPLETE GUIDE TO EDIBLE SAGO WORM FARMING

Sustainable Insect Protein Production, High-Yield Techniques, And Nutrient-Rich Cultivation Methods

GIOVANNI MALAKAI

© [2024] [Giovanni Malakai]. All rights reserved.

Except for brief quotations included in critical reviews and certain other noncommercial uses allowed by copyright law, no part of this publication may be reproduced, distributed, or transmitted in any form or by any means, including photocopying, recording, or other electronic or mechanical methods, without the publisher's prior written permission. Write to the publisher at the address below, addressing your letter to the "Attention: Permissions Coordinator," requesting permission.

DISCLAIMER

This book's content is solely intended for informational and educational purposes. The author and publisher of this book make no express or implied representations or warranties of any kind regarding the completeness, accuracy, reliability, suitability, or availability of the information, products, services, or related graphics contained in it, even though every effort has been made to ensure their accuracy and dependability. You consequently absolutely assume all risk associated with any reliance you may have on such material.

The author's own experiences and studies serve as the foundation for the techniques and procedures covered in this book. They might not be appropriate for every circumstance or person. Before putting any advice or recommendations from this book into practice, readers should use their own discretion and take into account their unique situation. Consulting with qualified professionals who specialize in veterinary care and animal management is always a good idea. Any direct, indirect, incidental or consequential damages resulting from using or relying on the material in this book are disclaimed by the author and publisher. Any decisions made by the reader based on the information presented herein are at their own risk.

TABLE OF CONTENTS

CHAPTER ONE 13
INTRODUCTION TO EDIBLE SAGO WORM FARMING 13
- EDIBLE SAGO WORMS: WHAT ARE THEY? 13
- WHY RAISE CONSUMABLE SAGO WORMS? 14
- THE ADVANTAGES OF RAISING EDIBLE SAGO WORMS 15
- COMPREHEND THE FARMING PROCEDURE 16
- HOW TO BEGIN GROWING EDIBLE SAGO WORMS 17

CHAPTER TWO 19
HOW TO ESTABLISH AN EDIBLE SAGO WORM FARM 19
- CHOOSING AN APPROPRIATE SITE 19
- BUILDING THE IDEAL WORM ENVIRONMENT 20
- SELECTING APPROPRIATE CONTAINERS 21
- FINDING HIGH-QUALITY SAGO PALM SUPPLIES 22
- INSTALLING THE FIRST FEEDING STATIONS 23

CHAPTER THREE 25
KNOWLEDGE OF EDIBLE SAGO WORMS 25
- THE SAGO WORM LIFE CYCLE 25
- DETERMINING WELL-BEING WORMS 26
- TRACING EXPANSION AND ADVANCEMENT 27
- CONTROLLING DENSITY OF POPULATION 28
- AVOIDING TYPICAL HEALTH PROBLEMS 29

CHAPTER FOUR 31
NUTRITION AND FEEDING OF EDIBLE SAGO WORMS 31
- THE GREATEST PLACES TO FIND SAGO WORM FOOD 31

    PREPARING HEALTHY FEED COMBINATIONS 32

    TIMETABLES FOR FEEDING AND AMOUNTS 34

    ADDING MINERALS AND VITAMINS AS SUPPLEMENTS 36

    MODIFYING DIET TO ACHIEVE IDEAL GROWTH 38

CHAPTER FIVE 41

  UPKEEP AND CONCERN 41

    UPKEEP AND CLEANING OF WORM CONTAINERS 41

    CONTROLLING HUMIDITY LEVELS 42

    INSULATION AND TEMPERATURE CONTROL 43

    TAKING CARE OF TRASH AND COMPOSTING 44

    CONSISTENT HEALTH EXAMINATIONS AND INSPECTIONS 45

CHAPTER SIX 47

  GATHERING CONGEALED SAGO WORMS 47

    INDICATIONS THAT IT'S TIME TO HARVEST 47

    COLLECTING METHODS THAT DON'T INJURE WORMS 48

    MANAGING COLLECTED WORMS 48

    SAGO WORM STORAGE AND PRESERVATION 49

    CONSUMPTION OR SALE PACKAGING 50

CHAPTER SEVEN 51

  HOW TO PROMOTE AND SELL YOUR EDIBLE SAGO WORMS 51

    FINDING THE RIGHT TARGET MARKETS 51

    PRODUCING PROMOTIONAL MATERIALS: 53

    PROFITABILITY-DRIVEN PRICING STRATEGIES: 54

    DISTRIBUTION AND SALES CHANNELS: 56

    DEVELOPING CONNECTIONS WITH CUSTOMERS: 57

CHAPTER EIGHT 59

TYPICAL ISSUES AND TROUBLESHOOTING 59

MANAGING VERMIN AND PREDATORS 59

RESOLVING ENVIRONMENTAL ISSUES 60

TAKING CARE OF WORM HEALTH CONCERNS 61

FIXING PROBLEMS RELATED TO GROWTH AND FEEDING 62

READINESS AND REACTION FOR EMERGENCIES 63

CHAPTER NINE 65

REGULATORY AND LEGAL ASPECTS 65

RECOGNIZING LICENSES AND PERMITS 65

ADHERENCE TO THE STANDARDS FOR HEALTH AND SAFETY 66

REGULATIONS FOR LABELING AND PACKAGING: 67

PROTECTION OF INTELLECTUAL PROPERTY 69

PRACTICES FOR ENVIRONMENTAL SUSTAINABILITY 70

CHAPTER TEN 73

FREQUENTLY ASKED QUESTIONS OR FAQS 73

ESTABLISHING A FARM FOR EDIBLE SAGO WORMS 73

THE GREATEST PLACES TO FIND SAGO WORM FOOD 74

SAGO WORM FEEDING FREQUENCY 75

INDICATIONS OF SOUND SAGO WORMS 76

INTERNATIONAL SAGO WORM SALES 77

CHAPTER ELEVEN 79

RESOURCES FOR ADDITIONAL EDUCATION 79

SUGGESTED READINGS AND SOURCES 79

FORUMS AND COMMUNITIES ONLINE 80

WORKSHOPS AND COURSES FOR TRAINING 81

EXPERT GUIDANCE & COACHING 83

ONGOING EDUCATION IN THE PRODUCTION OF SAGO 84

ABOUT THE BOOK

Offering priceless insights and detailed instructions for novice and seasoned farmers alike, the "Complete Guide to Edible Sago Worm Farming" is an all-inclusive manual created to maximize the potential of growing edible sago worms. Before delving into the world of these unusual animals, the guide explains the fundamentals, including what delicious sago worms are, why they are farmed, and the many advantages of doing so. Edible sago worm farming is a flexible and fruitful enterprise that can improve food security and support sustainable agriculture.

After that, the course moves smoothly into practical issues, starting with the important step of establishing your farm of tasty sago worms. We address every detail, from choosing the perfect spot to setting up an ideal atmosphere in appropriate containers. The primary focus is on locating premium sago palm resources and setting up productive feeding stations to efficiently initiate the farming process.

The life cycle of edible sago worms, health indicators, growth monitoring methods, population control tactics, and preventative steps against common health problems are all covered in detail after this. Equally enlightening on feeding and nutrition, which provides information on the finest food sources, nutrient-rich feed mixtures, feeding regimens, and dietary modifications for the best possible growth and development.

An additional crucial component of a successful sago worm farming operation is maintenance and care, which includes cleaning containers, controlling moisture, controlling temperature, handling waste, and doing routine health checks. Further discussion is provided on harvesting methods, which guarantee a smooth transfer from farm to table while preserving worm health.

The guide explores marketing and sales strategies for edible sago worms in addition to farming practices. In-depth research is done on target market identification, pricing strategies, sales channels, marketing tactics, and customer relationship building, enabling farmers to profitably market their yield in addition to producing it.

To ensure farm resilience and sustainability, common concerns and troubleshooting solutions offer important expertise in tackling obstacles such as pests, environmental factors, health issues, and crises. There is also a discussion of legal and regulatory issues, which helps farmers with licenses, compliance, labeling, and environmental stewardship.

The section on resources and further learning provides farmers with additional tools, suggested readings, online communities, training opportunities, and channels for professional advice, all of which promote ongoing development and proficiency in the field of edible sago worm farming. The Frequently Asked Questions (FAQs) anticipate and address frequently asked questions.

CHAPTER ONE

INTRODUCTION TO EDIBLE SAGO WORM FARMING

EDIBLE SAGO WORMS: WHAT ARE THEY?

Rhynchophorus ferrugineus, the scientific name for edible sago worms, are the larvae of the red palm weevil that are found in the sago palm's trunk. Because of the high protein content and nutritional worth of these worms, they have been enjoyed as a delicacy for ages in many different civilizations. They are regarded as an environmentally benign and sustainable source of protein in many places, particularly those where conventional cattle husbandry is not practical.

With their creamy-white underside and reddish-brown body, these worms are easily recognizable. They have a soft, plump feel and often reach a length of 5-7 cm. Though some people find them unpleasant at first, they are valued for their nutty taste and are frequently cooked in a variety of methods, such as frying, grilling, or adding them to soups and stews.

WHY RAISE CONSUMABLE SAGO WORMS?

Growing edible sago worms is a feasible alternative for people and communities trying to sustainably diversify their food sources because it has several benefits. First of all, they can be cultivated vertically and in tiny spaces, which makes them ideal for urban settings and small-scale businesses. In addition, they develop swiftly—maturing in only a few months—so when compared to other livestock, they may be harvested quickly.

Edible sago worms are a nutritious supplement to meals because of their high protein, good fat content, vitamins, and minerals content. This is especially true in areas where protein deficiencies are a problem. In addition to enhancing biodiversity and lessening the strain on conventional livestock resources, the cultivation of these worms supports sustainable methods of food production.

THE ADVANTAGES OF RAISING EDIBLE SAGO WORMS

Edible sago worm cultivation offers advantages beyond sustainability and nutritional value. From an economic standpoint, it can give farmers a source of income, particularly in rural areas where job possibilities could be few. The demand for edible insects is expanding worldwide, offering farmers the chance to meet this demand and broaden the scope of their farming operations.

In addition, sago palm trees—the host plant for these worms—are widely distributed in tropical areas, providing a readily available and replenishable source for agricultural purposes. Because of its accessibility and very low production costs as compared to conventional livestock, edible sago worm farming is a financially feasible choice for small-scale farmers and business owners.

COMPREHEND THE FARMING PROCEDURE

To ensure optimal growing and harvest, there are a few essential processes involved in edible sago worm farming. The first step is to find healthy sago palm trees that are devoid of chemicals and pesticides, as these can kill the worms. After the palm trees are found, they are examined to see whether any larvae are present. whether so, they are carefully collected to prevent any damage from occurring.

The larvae that have been gathered are then placed in trays or containers that have been properly made and filled with a substrate that resembles their natural home. Sago palm fibers, organic debris, and things that hold moisture are commonly found in this substrate, which helps to produce an environment that is favorable for the worms' growth. Throughout the farming process, it is essential to regularly monitor the temperature, humidity, and availability of food to promote the best possible growth and development.

The larvae go through phases of molting as they develop, losing their outer layer to make room for their growing bodies. To promote healthy growth during these periods, proper nutrition is crucial, which includes giving fresh sago palm leaves or other appropriate food sources. To prevent contamination, farmers must also control pests and diseases that could harm the worms and keep the agricultural area clean and hygienic.

HOW TO BEGIN GROWING EDIBLE SAGO WORMS

Research and knowledge of the farming procedure are crucial for those who want to start an edible sago worm farm. Understanding the nutritional needs of sago worms, their life cycle, and the environmental factors that promote their growth is essential. Joining regional agricultural organizations or asking seasoned farmers for advice can be a great way to get assistance and insightful information.

Finding appropriate sago palm trees to get larvae and setting up the farming area with the required tools and supplies are the first tasks. Achieving successful worm farming requires careful monitoring of the worms' development and the creation of a sustainable feeding plan. To maximize productivity and guarantee a healthy harvest, regular observation and modifications depending on environmental conditions and the behavior of the worms are required.

Beginners may create a profitable and sustainable business that supports food security, biodiversity conservation, and economic stability by adhering to best practices in edible sago worm farming.

CHAPTER TWO

HOW TO ESTABLISH AN EDIBLE SAGO WORM FARM

CHOOSING AN APPROPRIATE SITE

Choosing a good site is the first step in starting an edible sago worm farm. Seek out an area with some shade or indirect sunshine; the worms may find direct sunlight to be too intense. The worms' health depends on maintaining adequate airflow, so make sure the room is well-ventilated. The worms can become stressed by strong drafts or abrupt temperature changes, so keep the farm away from these conditions.

Select a spot that is best suited for routine maintenance chores like feeding and harvesting. To shield the farm from rain and excessive moisture, think about putting it in a shed, garage, or covered outside space. Steer clear of places with heavy machinery or chemical storage since they could bring toxins that are bad for the worms.

You can establish a favorable habitat for the sago worms to live and procreate by choosing the ideal place.

BUILDING THE IDEAL WORM ENVIRONMENT

After deciding on a spot, concentrate on setting up your sago worms' ideal habitat. Prepare the bedding material first. Shredded cardboard, coconut coir, and organic compost can all be used to make this. In addition to giving the worms a nourishing substrate to eat, this encourages microbial activity, which is necessary for their digestion.

To keep the bedding from getting excessively dry or soggy, keep the moisture content at a level comparable to that of a wrung-out sponge. The ideal temperature range for the growth and reproduction of sago worms is 75–85°F (24–29°C), so keep an eye on it. To keep stability, use a thermometer to measure the temperature frequently and modify the insulation or airflow as necessary.

Cover the containers with a permeable cloth or lid with ventilation holes to create a dark and silent habitat. In addition to lowering stress and simulating their natural habitat, this helps the worms feed and procreate more effectively. You may create the ideal conditions for a healthy sago worm culture by setting up the right atmosphere.

SELECTING APPROPRIATE CONTAINERS

Your edible sago worm farm's success depends on your choice of containers. Choose receptacles that provide adequate room for the worms' growth and mobility. Wooden boxes or plastic bins with lids are good options for insulation and weather protection.

Make sure there are drainage holes in the containers to avoid waterlogging and let extra moisture out. To enhance drainage and avoid compacting the bedding material, place a layer of gravel or small stones at the bottom of the containers. This keeps the worms' surroundings healthy and encourages aeration.

When selecting containers, take into account how simple they will be to clean and maintain. You will need to replace the bedding material and remove trash regularly. To maintain track of feeding schedules and track the worms' progress, label the containers appropriately. Selecting the appropriate containers simplifies management duties and lays the groundwork for productive sago worm farming.

FINDING HIGH-QUALITY SAGO PALM SUPPLIES

Finding high-quality sago palm resources is a crucial component of starting an edible sago worm farm. Use newly collected, responsibly farmed sago palm logs or trunks, ideally free of pesticides. Recycled or chemically tainted palm materials should not be used as they can damage worms and hinder their development and reproduction.

Cut the sago palm materials into appropriate lengths and remove any extra bark or debris to prepare them. To soften and increase their palatability for the worms, soak the palm portions in water for several days. Moreover, this procedure aids in the removal of tannins and other substances that can be hazardous to the worms.

Before adding the sago palm materials to the worm farm, check them for indications of mold, bugs, or deterioration. To guarantee that the worms have access to wholesome and secure food sources, only use clean and healthy palm pieces. For the worms to grow and develop to their full potential, you must supply vital nutrients and promote their feeding habit by obtaining high-quality sago palm materials.

INSTALLING THE FIRST FEEDING STATIONS

It's time to set up your sago worms' first feeding stations after everything is ready. After the sago palm sections are soaked and ready, place them in the containers so the worms can easily access them for feeding. To give the worms a cozy surface and aid in moisture retention, lightly cover the palm portions with the bedding material.

Make sure there is a sufficient quantity of food for the worms by routinely checking on the feeding stations. To keep things clean and avoid odor accumulation, add fresh palm sections as needed and eliminate any uneaten or decayed material. To prevent overfeeding or underfeeding, modify the feeding frequency by the worms' rate of consumption and the surrounding circumstances.

Maintain a feeding journal to record the quantity and quality of food given as well as behavioral and health observations about the worms. By doing this, feeding procedures may be improved and adequate nourishment for the worms' healthy growth can be guaranteed. Your sago worm farm's initial feeding station setup lays the groundwork for continued worm care and cultivation.

CHAPTER THREE

KNOWLEDGE OF EDIBLE SAGO WORMS

THE SAGO WORM LIFE CYCLE

For farming to be effective, one must comprehend the sago worm life cycle. The female moth lays its eggs on the leaves of particular palm trees, and that is where it all starts. The tiny, nearly invisible larvae that emerge from these eggs are seen with the naked eye. After that, the larvae tunnel into the palm tree's stem, where they eat and develop. Several months may pass during this phase, depending on several variables like the availability of food and the temperature.

The larvae go through multiple molting stages as they develop, losing their exoskeleton to make room for their growing bodies. When the larvae are fully grown, they pupate within the tree. They go through metamorphosis and become adult moths during this pupal stage. After emerging from the tree to mate, adult moths laid eggs to restart the cycle.

Farmers can better organize their farming activities by anticipating the timing of various stages when they have a thorough understanding of this cycle.

DETERMINING WELL-BEING WORMS

Knowing which worms are healthy is crucial to running a profitable sago worm farm. Sago worms in good health are usually creamy-white in color and plump. When touched, they ought to be lively and receptive, moving with ease and displaying no symptoms of discomfort. Their skin needs to be flawless and devoid of any lesions that can point to an illness or infection.

The hunger and feeding habits of the sago worms are another indication of their health. When worms are in good health, they will eat a lot of palm tissue and leave the stem with clean tunnels. Additionally, they need to excrete regularly, which suggests healthy metabolism and digestion. Regular inspection and knowledge of what to look for will help you spot problems like sickness, stress, or malnourishment in your worm population and take the necessary steps to keep it healthy.

TRACING EXPANSION AND ADVANCEMENT

To maximize the productivity of sago worms, it is essential to keep an eye on their growth and development. This entails taking consistent measurements of important factors like size, weight, and developmental stage. Farmers can detect anomalies or development retardation at an early stage using growth tracking, which may be a sign of health problems or environmental stressors.

Moreover, tracking development entails keeping an eye on activities including eating habits, molting frequency, and pupation. These observations shed important light on the worms' general health and well-being. Farmers may maximize the quantity and quality of their sago worms by keeping thorough records and observing patterns over time.

This allows them to make educated decisions about feeding schedules, environmental factors, and harvesting timetables.

CONTROLLING DENSITY OF POPULATION

An effective population density control program is necessary to keep the sago worm farm healthy and productive. Competition for resources like food and space brought on by overcrowding can lead to stunted growth, elevated stress levels, and increased illness susceptibility. Conversely, low population density can result in the underuse of available space and inefficient use of resources.

Farmers should routinely measure the number of worms per unit area and modify stocking levels as necessary to efficiently manage population density. To maintain ideal conditions for growth and development, this may entail relocating worms or thinning out dense areas. A balanced and healthy sago worm population is maintained through proactive response and monitoring of population dynamics.

AVOIDING TYPICAL HEALTH PROBLEMS

For a sago worm farm to be successful over the long run, common health risks must be avoided. Infection is one of the main health risks, and it can be brought on by contaminated food sources, poor hygiene, or crowded living conditions. Farming facilities and equipment can reduce the risk of illness by being cleaned and disinfected regularly.

Malnutrition is another prevalent health problem that can be brought on by insufficient or unbalanced diets. Nutritional deficits can be avoided by ensuring that sago worms have access to nutrient-rich food sources like freshly cut palm tissue or properly prepared diets. Furthermore, keeping an eye on environmental factors like humidity and temperature might assist in identifying possible stressors that may be linked to health problems.

Overall, preventing common health issues and preserving healthy sago worm farm need a proactive approach to health management that includes routine inspections, good hygiene procedures, and a suitable diet.

CHAPTER FOUR

NUTRITION AND FEEDING OF EDIBLE SAGO WORMS

THE GREATEST PLACES TO FIND SAGO WORM FOOD

Like many other insect species, sago worms are fed a wide range of naturally occurring foods that are high in nutrients and necessary for their development. Decomposing wood, particularly that from palm trees, is one of the main food sources for sago worms. Sago worms thrive in the soft, moist texture of decomposing palm wood, which is ideal for their growth and feeding. Fruits with a high sugar content and nutritional value, including papayas and bananas, are also great options for a sago worm diet. These fruits can be cut into slices and added to the worm farm so the worms have easy access to them.

Rich in protein and carbs, rice bran is another excellent food source for sago worms. It is easier for the worms to ingest rice bran if it is combined with a little water to make a wet paste. Vegetables such as sweet potatoes, carrots, and pumpkins can also be grated or finely chopped and put to the worm farm as additional food sources. In addition to offering the worms vital nutrients, these veggies vary their diet and encourage the worms' normal growth and development.

Furthermore, because they contain vitamins and minerals that are essential to sago worms' general health, leafy greens like lettuce, spinach, and kale are good for them. To provide the worms with a healthy diet cut these greens finely and combine them with different food sources. All things considered, feeding sago worms a varied and nutrient-rich diet that is necessary for their optimum growth and development involves adding a blend of fruits, vegetables, rice bran, decaying wood, and leafy greens.

PREPARING HEALTHY FEED COMBINATIONS

To provide sago worms with a balanced diet that satisfies their nutritional needs, a variety of food sources are combined to create nutritious feed mixtures.

Rice bran, a range of fruits and vegetables, and decomposing palm wood can make up a basic sago worm diet. To begin, gather decaying palm wood from palm trees or purchase it from nearby vendors. To make it easier for the worms to eat, break, or shred the palm wood into little pieces.

Then, to make the base for the feed mix, combine the rice bran and the shredded palm wood. The palm wood offers texture and fiber, and the rice bran supplies protein and carbohydrates. Chopped fruits such as apples, bananas, and papayas can be added to the mixture to increase its nutritional content and sweetness. To improve the feed mix's nutrient value, add veggies like sweet potatoes, carrots, and leafy greens like spinach and lettuce.

To make the meal mix more appealing to the worms, it is imperative to keep it moist. Little additions of water or frequent misting of the mixture with water keep it moist and make it simpler for the sago worms to consume.

By combining rice bran, fruits, vegetables, decaying palm wood, and other nutritional ingredients, you may make a feed mix that gives sago worms a balanced diet that supports their healthy growth and development.

TIMETABLES FOR FEEDING AND AMOUNTS

Setting up appropriate feeding schedules and amounts is essential to keeping sago worms healthy and productive in a worm farm. Regular feeding is necessary to guarantee that sago worms have an appropriate quantity of nutrients for growth. Depending on the worms' hunger and the quantity of food they eat at each feeding session, it is advised to feed them every two to three days.

It's critical to keep an eye on the amount of food given to sago worms to prevent overfeeding, which can result in waste accumulation and possible health problems for the worms. To begin, give the worms a small quantity of meal mix, and watch how rapidly they eat it.

Depending on how hungry they are, adjust the amount of food they are fed to make sure they complete it in an acceptable amount of time.

When calculating feeding quantities, keep the size of the worm population in mind as well. While a smaller population can survive on smaller portions, a greater population would need more food. Additionally, it is advantageous to equally distribute the feed mix throughout the worm farm to guarantee that every worm has access to food and avoid worm congestion in particular places.

Determine the frequency and amount of feedings based on the sago worms' activity and development rates. When the worms get older and their nutritional requirements alter, adjustments can be required. The health and productivity of sago worms in your worm farm can be maximized by setting up a regular feeding plan and keeping an eye on feeding amounts.

ADDING MINERALS AND VITAMINS AS SUPPLEMENTS

Vitamins and minerals must be added to the diet of sago worms to guarantee that they get all the nutrition required for healthy growth. Even while a variety of vital elements are naturally found in foods including fruits, vegetables, and decomposing wood, supplementing their diet can further improve their nutritional worth. Supplements containing vitamins and minerals are offered in a variety of formats, such as liquids and powders that are intended for ingestion by insects.

Calcium is an essential supplement for sago worms since it is necessary for the growth of their exoskeleton and general health. Crushed eggshells or commercial calcium powder intended for insects are two ways to supply calcium. To make sure the worms get enough food, sprinkle a tiny bit of calcium supplement over the meal mix before serving it to them.

Vitamin D3, which aids in the efficient metabolism of calcium by sago worms, is another crucial supplement. Supplements containing vitamin D3 should be given either independently or in combination with the diet mix, according to the prescribed dosage for invertebrates. Moreover, think about adding multivitamin pills made just for insects to supply an extensive array of vital vitamins and minerals.

Sago worms may be harmed by excessive vitamin and mineral supplementation, therefore it's important to go by dose recommendations and refrain from over-supplementing. After adding supplements, keep an eye on the worms' development and health to make sure the extra nutrients are beneficial to them and don't have any negative consequences. You may encourage ideal growth, development, and general health in your sago worm farm by adding vitamins and minerals to their diet.

MODIFYING DIET TO ACHIEVE IDEAL GROWTH

Sago worms' diets must be carefully adjusted for optimal growth, taking into account their developmental stages and the conditions of their surroundings when determining the best food sources and nutritional intake. The nutritional needs of sago worms vary as they develop from larvae to pupae and finally adults, necessitating modifications to the makeup of their diet. Comprehending these feeding modifications is crucial to optimize their development potential and efficiency in a worm farm environment.

Sago worms need a diet high in proteins, carbs, and lipids during their larval stage to support their rapid growth and development. To help them achieve their energy demands, provide protein-rich food sources like rice bran and decomposing wood, as well as supplemental supplies like mealworms or fish meals. To encourage effective feeding, make sure the larval food is readily accessible and quickly digested.

When sago worms reach the pupal stage, their diet changes to concentrate on storing energy for when they change into adults. To gain sustained energy without consuming too much protein, change the diet to include more foods high in carbohydrates, such as fruits and vegetables.

Restricting protein intake during the pupal stage helps avoid overgrowth and guarantees healthy transformation into adult sago worms.

Sago worms' nutritional requirements stabilize as they get older, with an emphasis on a diet that is balanced and includes a variety of proteins, carbs, vitamins, and minerals. Maintain providing a varied diet consisting of fruits, vegetables, natural food sources like decomposing wood, and extra nutrients as needed. To fine-tune their food for optimal growth and productivity throughout their life cycle, keep an eye on their growth rate, reproductive activity, and general health.

You may promote sago worms' growth, development, and reproductive success in a worm farm setting by modifying their diet according to their developmental phases and nutritional needs. Check their nutrition frequently and adjust it as necessary to make sure they get the nutrients needed for strong development and general well-being.

CHAPTER FIVE

UPKEEP AND CONCERN

UPKEEP AND CLEANING OF WORM CONTAINERS

Successful edible sago worm farming depends on keeping your worm containers clean and well-maintained. Start by carefully cleaning the containers with a mild soap solution, emptying them regularly, and removing any residual food. Before adding more new bedding material to the containers, give them a thorough rinse to get rid of any leftover material. This maintains your worms' surroundings healthy and helps stop the growth of dangerous germs.

Furthermore, make sure to routinely check the containers for any indications of mildew, vermin, or other problems that can be harmful to the worms' health. If you find any issues, deal with them right away by treating the containers with natural pest control solutions or removing any impacted bedding. Maintaining a clean and well-maintained container can help your sago worms grow and develop to their full potential.

CONTROLLING HUMIDITY LEVELS

Your sago worms' health depends on maintaining the proper moisture levels. While too little moisture can result in dehydration and impede the growth of the worms, too much moisture can promote the growth of mold and germs. Make sure the bedding material is damp but not too wet to properly control the amount of moisture present. Mist the bedding as needed with a spray bottle to keep it moist but not soggy.

To help control moisture levels, you can also incorporate moisture-retaining materials into the bedding, such as coconut coir or shredded newspaper. It is important to periodically check the moisture content and make any required modifications, particularly in dry or humid weather. Your worms will feel more at ease and be healthier and more productive if you control the moisture in the environment.

INSULATION AND TEMPERATURE CONTROL

The success of your edible sago worm farm depends on maintaining ideal temperatures. The ideal temperature range for sago worms is between 25°C and 30°C (77°F and 86°F).

To shield the worms from sharp temperature swings, make sure the farming area is adequately insulated. Styrofoam or insulating blankets can be used to establish a stable atmosphere within the containers.

To avoid overheating in hot weather, offer shade or make use of fans. Use heating pads or heat lamps in colder climates to keep the desired temperature range. To guarantee the comfort and well-being of your sago worms, periodically check the temperature within the containers and make any necessary adjustments. Healthy development and reproduction rates are supported by appropriate temperature regulation.

TAKING CARE OF TRASH AND COMPOSTING

Effective waste management is essential to the production of edible sago worms. The worms make nutrient-rich castings that are good for the health of the soil as they eat organic debris. Worm castings can be collected regularly and used as compost for your gardens or plants. This not only lowers waste but also enhances soil fertility and encourages environmentally friendly farming methods.

Additionally, to keep the worm containers clean and avoid odor accumulation, remove any undigested food or waste. To filter out any debris from the castings, use a sieve or mesh screen. You can recycle nutrients and make a nutrient-rich soil amendment for your plants by composting the waste material in a separate bin or compost pile. Sustainable farming methods and a robust ecosystem are enhanced by effective waste management.

CONSISTENT HEALTH EXAMINATIONS AND INSPECTIONS

It is imperative to conduct routine health checks and inspections to ensure the well-being of your sago worms. Visually inspect the worms frequently to look for indications of illness, stress, or parasites. As markers of general health, look for normal food habits, active mobility, and healthy coloring.

Take prompt action to address any anomalies or symptoms of sickness that you observe. Take any ill or damaged worms out of the containers and give them the proper attention. To monitor your worm population's health and progress over time, keep track of your observations and health checks.

In summary, the secret to successful edible sago worm farming is to prioritize cleaning and maintenance, control temperatures, manage moisture levels, correctly handle waste, and do routine health checks.

Through adherence to these rules and continual observation of your worms' requirements, you may establish a healthy and long-lasting worm farming environment.

CHAPTER SIX
GATHERING CONGEALED SAGO WORMS
INDICATIONS THAT IT'S TIME TO HARVEST

There are a few telltale indicators that indicate when it's time to harvest your edible sago worms. Look at the worms' color first. The characteristic creamy white or light beige hue of mature worms indicates that they are ready to be harvested. The size of the worms is another indicator; adult worms are typically as thick as a pencil and measure between five and seven centimeters in length.

Furthermore, search the substrate for worms that are actively moving. Their level of harvest preparedness can be inferred from this movement. Additionally, mature worms will appear plump, which is a sign that they are nutrient-rich. Finally, worms are ready to be harvested if you see them attempting to climb the walls of their container or flee the substrate.

COLLECTING METHODS THAT DON'T INJURE WORMS

To harvest tasty sago worms without injuring the worms, meticulous methods must be followed. Using a tiny shovel or spoon, start by gradually removing the substrate surrounding the worms. To prevent crushing or harming the worms, do not handle them directly with your hands. To reveal the worms beneath, gradually raise the substrate.

Next, gently extract the worms from the substrate using your fingers or a gentle brush. Try not to pull or tug on the worms; this can harm them, so be patient. Instead, encourage them to come out on their own by applying light pressure. After the worms have been removed from the substrate, place them in a sterile container to be processed.

MANAGING COLLECTED WORMS

It's crucial to correctly prepare the sago worms after gathering them to make sure they're safe to eat. To begin, give the worms a gentle rinse under cold water to get rid of any dirt or debris from their bodies. Use caution while using boiling water to avoid overcooking the worms.

Next, look for any indications of deterioration or injury on the worms. Any worms that seem sick or discolored should be thrown away. After the worms have been cleaned and examined, you can prepare them using the recipe of your choice.

Make sure they are cooked through, whether you're boiling, frying, or adding them to a recipe. This will help to minimize any dangers.

SAGO WORM STORAGE AND PRESERVATION

Edible sago worms must be stored and preserved properly to retain their quality and freshness. After collecting, store the worms in a cool, dry location out of direct sunlight if you won't be using them right away. To keep the worms safe from pollutants and moisture, you can use ziplock bags or airtight containers.

You might want to freeze the worms for longer-term storage. Transfer them to a baking sheet in a single layer, then freeze for firmness. After they're frozen, move them to a freezer-safe bag or container and keep them there. Sago worms that are frozen can be kept for several months without becoming less tasty.

CONSUMPTION OR SALE PACKAGING

Hygiene and presentation are crucial factors to take into account when packing edible sago worms for sale or eating. Make use of hygienic, food-grade packing materials, including plastic containers or bags. Make sure the package is well sealed to keep freshness and avoid contamination.

If you are selling the worms, you might want to write important information on the box, like the date of harvest, how to store them, and any pertinent nutritional information. Customers will receive useful information from this, and your goods will appear more professional.

CHAPTER SEVEN

HOW TO PROMOTE AND SELL YOUR EDIBLE SAGO WORMS

FINDING THE RIGHT TARGET MARKETS

Finding your target consumers is the first step towards effectively marketing and selling your delicious sago worms. Start by learning about the tastes and demographics of possible clients who are considering sustainable protein sources or edible insects. Take into account variables like age, way of life, food choices, and environmental awareness. Your target market may include people who are looking for eco-friendly food options, adventurous eaters, and health-conscious individuals.

Next, divide up your target markets according to their unique requirements and inclinations. This can entail making distinctions between retail customers, eateries or food service providers, and marketplaces or specialty shops that focus on unusual food items.

Gather information on what influences their purchasing decisions and how they view edible sago worms as a food product by conducting surveys, interviews, or market research. You may better satisfy the demands and pique the interest of your target market by customizing your marketing methods and product offers based on an understanding of their motivations and preferences.

Create focused marketing campaigns and tactics to effectively reach your target markets after you have determined who they are and how to segment them. To target particular audience segments, make use of digital marketing channels like social media, internet platforms, and tailored advertising. Work together with nutritionists, chefs, and influencers who can tell your target audiences about the culinary applications and health advantages of eating sago worms. To improve your marketing strategies and adapt to shifting consumer wants and preferences, keep a close eye on market trends and customer feedback.

PRODUCING PROMOTIONAL MATERIALS:

To advertise your tasty sago worms and draw in new clients, you must create eye-catching marketing collateral. Create a brand identity first that captures the special features and advantages of your offering. Creating a logo, packaging, and other visual components that communicate the nutritive value, sustainability, and culinary adaptability of edible sago worms is part of this. Make use of top-notch photos and graphics to present the goods in the best possible way and pique the interest of your intended market.

Create interesting and educational content for your website, product descriptions, and promotional materials, among other marketing materials. To inform and convince potential buyers, emphasize the edible sago worms' nutritional advantages, culinary applications, and sustainability. By illustrating the journey from farm to table and highlighting the natural and environmentally friendly manufacturing processes, you can establish a relationship with your audience through the use of storytelling tactics.

Make use of a multi-channel marketing strategy to increase exposure and outreach. Use email marketing, blogs, social media, and conventional advertising methods to effectively promote your brand's message and product offerings. To establish credibility and trust, include client recommendations, reviews, and testimonials. Maintain the relevance and appeal of your marketing materials for your target audience by updating and refreshing them frequently to reflect new developments and consumer preferences in the food business.

PROFITABILITY-DRIVEN PRICING STRATEGIES:

Creating strategies for pricing that work is essential to maintaining profitability while competing in the market. To start, figure out the production costs of edible sago worms, including farming, processing, packing, and marketing costs.

This can be done by performing a comprehensive cost analysis. Consider labor costs, overhead, and any capital expenditures for technology or equipment required for farming and processing.

While determining the price of your products, take into account pricing trends, competition, and market demand. Assess the target market's perception of the value of edible sago worms and ascertain price elasticity to comprehend the potential effects of price fluctuations on demand. To determine the best price points that strike a balance between profitability and customer affordability, use pricing models like cost-plus pricing, value-based pricing, or competitive pricing.

Use price tactics that promote repeat business, large purchases, or loyalty programs to keep customers and increase sales. Provide bundles or pricing levels that cater to certain customer segments according to their inclinations and buying patterns. To be profitable and competitive over time, keep an eye on market dynamics and make necessary adjustments to pricing plans, taking into account things like supply chain costs, seasonal variations, and general economic conditions.

DISTRIBUTION AND SALES CHANNELS:

Reaching your target markets and optimizing sales potential for edible sago worms depends on selecting the appropriate sales channels and distribution strategies. To identify the best sales channels, start by evaluating the tastes and purchasing patterns of your target market. This could take the shape of collaborations with distributors and wholesalers, wholesale distribution to retailers and food service providers, or direct-to-consumer sales via your website or online marketplace platforms.

Create a thorough sales and distribution plan that specifies the obligations of each channel partner and guarantees constant product availability and quality at all points of contact. To extend your market reach and gain access to new client segments, cultivate relationships with retailers, important distribution partners, and other industry stakeholders in the food sector. When designing your distribution network, take into account inventory management, logistics, and geographic factors to maximize effectiveness and save expenses.

Make use of digital tools and technology to manage inventories, track sales performance across channels, and expedite sales procedures. To ensure smooth transactions and consumer interactions, put online ordering platforms, inventory management software, and e-commerce capabilities into place. As consumer preferences and industry dynamics change, you can find possibilities for growth and development in your sales and distribution strategy by keeping an eye on sales data, customer feedback, and market trends.

DEVELOPING CONNECTIONS WITH CUSTOMERS:

Marketing and selling delicious sago worms successfully requires you to establish enduring relationships with your clients.

Begin by learning about the requirements, inclinations, and opinions of your clients using market research, questionnaires, and direct client communications. To exceed their expectations and cultivate loyalty, use this knowledge to customize your marketing messages, product offerings, and customer service encounters.

Provide interesting and educational content that informs readers about the culinary applications, sustainability, and nutritional advantages of edible sago worms. Offer a variety of recipes, culinary advice, and serving ideas to encourage your clientele's imagination and creative use. Use blogs, newsletters, and social media to interact with customers, provide news and promotions, and ask for comments and evaluations.

Provide outstanding customer support and assistance to answer questions, fix problems, and guarantee a happy purchasing experience. Use customer retention techniques to encourage recurring business and build enduring relationships with your clientele, such as loyalty programs, special offers, and discounts.

CHAPTER EIGHT

TYPICAL ISSUES AND TROUBLESHOOTING

MANAGING VERMIN AND PREDATORS

Managing pests and predators that could harm your worm population is one of the main concerns in delicious sago worm cultivation. Among the common pests that can harm worm bins are mites, beetles, and ants. It's crucial to often check your worm bins for any indications of infestation to fight against these pests. Without endangering your worms, you can control pest populations by employing natural pest control techniques like applying neem oil or importing predatory insects.

Your sago worms may also be threatened by rodents, birds, and other small creatures. Think about erecting physical barriers, like wire mesh or fence, around your worm bins to keep predators away. Additionally, by giving your worms enough shelter and reducing their exposure to possible predators, you may establish a safe habitat for them.

RESOLVING ENVIRONMENTAL ISSUES

Environmental factors that can affect your sago worms' growth and health include temperature swings, humidity, and exposure to sunshine. For the worms in your bins to stay healthy, the circumstances must always be at their best. Maintain stable temperatures between 20 and 30 degrees Celsius and humidity levels between 60 and 80% for your worm bins by keeping them in a shaded place.

Keep a frequent eye on the moisture content of your worm bins to keep them from getting too dry or wet. For your worms to stay comfortable and at the right moisture level, use bedding materials like shredded newspaper or coconut coir. Maintaining your worms' oxygen levels and preventing the accumulation of hazardous gasses depend on proper ventilation.

TAKING CARE OF WORM HEALTH CONCERNS

Sustaining your sago worms' health is essential to agricultural success. Fungal growth, dietary deficiencies, and bacterial infections are common health problems. Check your worms frequently for anomalies or symptoms of disease, such as discoloration, sluggishness, or strange behavior. Remove sick or infected worms from your worm population to stop the disease from spreading.

Give your worms a well-balanced diet of fruits, vegetables, and leaves from the sago palm, which are high in minerals like calcium, protein, and carbs. Steer clear of overfeeding your worms because this might promote bacterial growth and other health issues. Maintaining good sanitation and hygiene, such as routinely cleaning worm bins and clearing away waste accumulation, will also help keep your sago worms healthy.

FIXING PROBLEMS RELATED TO GROWTH AND FEEDING

Sago worm farming might experience feeding and growth problems as a result of poor diet, environmental conditions, or medical conditions. Examine your worm population's nutrition and diet if you observe low rates of reproduction or delayed growth. To make sure they get the vital nutrients for growth and development, change their feeding schedule and offer a range of food choices.

To establish the ideal environment for feeding and growth, keep an eye on the temperature, humidity, and moisture content in your worm bins. Refrain from packing your worm bins too full as this may result in competition for food and insufficient room for worm growth. Examine your worms' health and behavior regularly to spot any feeding or growth problems early and take quick corrective action.

READINESS AND REACTION FOR EMERGENCIES

In sago worm farming, emergency preparedness is essential to reducing potential dangers and guaranteeing the security of your worm population. Create an emergency response plan with procedures for handling illness outbreaks, natural disasters, and equipment malfunctions. Have backup food supplies, water bottles, and first aid kits on hand in case of emergency.

Examine your worm bins and infrastructure regularly to find any possible risks or weaknesses. Put preventive measures into action by strengthening buildings, locking down machinery, and performing routine maintenance inspections. To respond quickly and efficiently in emergencies, teach yourself and your team emergency procedures and response protocols.

CHAPTER NINE

REGULATORY AND LEGAL ASPECTS

RECOGNIZING LICENSES AND PERMITS

It's important to comprehend licenses and permits before beginning your tasty sago worm growing endeavor. First, learn about the particular laws and rules governing farming and food production in your state or nation. Usually, this entails acquiring permits from local government agencies or agricultural departments. Usually, these permits address things like food safety regulations, animal husbandry, and land use.

Next, think about any specific licenses required for the cultivation of edible sago worms. Depending on how you set things up, this could include permits for food processing or animal breeding. You must be aware of the licensing requirements, the application procedure, and any associated costs.

Ensuring compliance with these legal criteria guarantees the legitimacy and safety of your farming operations.

The license and permission procedure can also be streamlined by keeping abreast of regulatory changes and by keeping lines of communication open with the appropriate authorities. You support the general integrity of the food production industry by protecting your company and upholding these regulatory frameworks.

ADHERENCE TO THE STANDARDS FOR HEALTH AND SAFETY

Setting high priority for health and safety regulations is crucial when starting an edible sago worm farming operation. Start by applying strict cleanliness procedures to every aspect of your farming business. This entails keeping worm cultivation clean and under control, regularly sterilizing equipment, and managing waste.

Additionally, follow the guidelines established by regulatory agencies for food safety.

This entails preserving the ideal environments for worm growth, which include suitable humidity levels, temperature regulation, and sufficient feeding. To assist reduce hazards and guarantee the production of safe, high-quality worms, regular monitoring and testing for impurities or pathogens is recommended.

Compliance initiatives also benefit from staff workers' receiving health and safety best practices training and instruction. Stress the value of using personal protective equipment (PPE), safe handling practices, and hygienic measures to reduce risks and adhere to industry requirements. By putting health and safety first, you build a reliable and long-lasting farming operation.

REGULATIONS FOR LABELING AND PACKAGING:

Comprehending labeling and packaging requirements is essential for maintaining product integrity and fostering consumer trust in the field of edible sago worm farming. Learn about the criteria that food safety agencies have set for labeling.

Accurate product details including ingredients, nutritional value, expiration dates, and allergen alerts are included in this.

Invest in environmentally sustainable packaging materials that meet your sustainability targets and maintain the freshness and quality of your products. Make sure that packaging designs adhere to branding standards and provide consumers with the necessary information. Use barcodes and QR codes on labels to increase product transparency and traceability.

Review and update labeling and packaging procedures regularly to take into account changes in industry standards or regulations.

If necessary, consult labeling specialists or consultants to guarantee compliance and maximize consumer appeal. You build trust and confidence in your edible sago worm goods by following these guidelines.

PROTECTION OF INTELLECTUAL PROPERTY

Intellectual property protection is essential for innovation and competition in the edible sago worm farming industry. Start by noting down any special farming approaches, breeding strategies, or product formulas that you create. To protect your innovations, think about speaking with intellectual property lawyers about your choices for copyrights, trademarks, and patents.

When working with suppliers, partners, or researchers, make sure to implement non-disclosure agreements (NDAs) or confidentiality agreements to avoid the illegal use or distribution of private information. Review and adjust your intellectual property strategy frequently to keep up with changing market conditions and advances in technology.

Keep an eye out for possible infringements or unlawful usage of your intellectual property by conducting continual market research and monitoring. To protect your rights and keep a competitive edge in the edible sago worm farming market, be ready to go to court if needed. By taking proactive measures to safeguard your intellectual property, you put yourself up for long-term prosperity and creativity.

PRACTICES FOR ENVIRONMENTAL SUSTAINABILITY

Adopting environmental sustainability methods is crucial for ecological stewardship and long-term survival in the context of edible sago worm farming. Begin by evaluating how your farming practices affect the environment in terms of resource consumption, waste production, and ecosystem health. Throughout your business, put policies in place to cut down on waste, preserve water, and lower your carbon impact.

To enhance biodiversity and soil health, investigate sustainable agricultural methods like integrated pest management (IPM), organic farming, and permaculture concepts. To improve sustainability and resilience in your farming practices, include natural pest management techniques, efficient irrigation systems, and renewable energy sources.

Practice sustainable sourcing when obtaining inputs, like feedstock or substrate materials, giving local vendors and environmentally friendly substitutes priority. Use consumer education programs, eco-certifications, and transparent labeling to demonstrate your commitment to environmental sustainability. Work together with groups or specialists in sustainability to continuously innovate and enhance your farming methods for a more environmentally friendly future.

CHAPTER TEN

FREQUENTLY ASKED QUESTIONS OR FAQS

ESTABLISHING A FARM FOR EDIBLE SAGO WORMS

You need a suitable container, such as a wooden box or plastic tub with a lid to keep the worms contained, to start an edible sago worm farm. Make sure the lid has tiny ventilation holes. Next, use shredded newspaper or wet coconut husks to make a bedding layer. The worms are given a cozy environment as a result.

Obtain logs or stems from sago palms; fresh is best since sago worms feed mostly on these. After chopping the logs, arrange them in the container. To feed and procreate, the worms will naturally go to the logs.

To get your farm started, introduce a small number of sago worms and make sure they have access to enough food and moisture. The best conditions for sago worm growth and reproduction are shade and a temperature of 25 to 30 degrees Celsius, so keep the container there.

Check the moisture content frequently, and if the bedding seems dry, add water.

THE GREATEST PLACES TO FIND SAGO WORM FOOD

Fresh sago palm logs or stems are ideal for sago worm growth. These ought to be your worm farm's primary feeding supply. Make sure the logs are clean, fresh, and devoid of any chemicals or pesticides that can hurt the worms. To make the logs fit in your container cut them into small pieces.

Mangos, papayas, and bananas are a few more fruits that provide good food sources. They may occasionally be provided these to add variety and to enhance their nutrition. Citrus fruits should not be given to them since they may be too acidic for the worms.

Make sure the worms have access to new food by rotating the sago palm logs regularly. The worms can be harmed by dirty, decomposing, or moldy feeding sources.

Proper maintenance and a varied diet will ensure that your sago worms grow to be robust and healthy.

SAGO WORM FEEDING FREQUENCY

Regular feeding is necessary to keep sago worms healthy and growing. Feeding can be done every two to three days, depending on the size and quantity of worms in your worm farm. Keep an eye on how much they eat and make adjustments as necessary.

As the primary food source, provide fresh sago palm logs or stems, making sure they eat enough without being overfed. Refrain from overcrowding the container as this may draw pests and lead to pollution.

Increase the frequency of feedings if you observe that the worms are devouring the food rapidly or exhibiting signs of hunger. On the other hand, cut back on the amount provided if there is leftover food after a day to avoid waste and maintain a clean workplace.

INDICATIONS OF SOUND SAGO WORMS

Sago worms in good health display specific traits that signify their well-being. Their bodies should be robust and fat, and they should respond quickly when startled. They should be creamy white or light brown in hue, devoid of any odd marks or evidence of deterioration.

Make sure the bedding is consistently damp but not soggy by checking its moisture content regularly. To exhibit interest in their food source, healthy worms will burrow into the bedding and feed on the sago palm logs.

Keep an eye on their pace of reproduction and growth. A prosperous farm is shown by healthy worms that grow steadily and generate offspring. As soon as you see any anomalies or disease-related symptoms, such as fatigue or discoloration, act to resolve the problem and stop its progression.

INTERNATIONAL SAGO WORM SALES

It is feasible to sell sago worms abroad as long as the right paperwork is submitted and rules are followed. To guarantee adherence to international standards, find out what your country's legal requirements are for exporting live insects.

Obtain the permissions or permits required to export live sago worms. Agriculture officials may conduct inspections to verify the worms' health and export-suitability.

Enclose the sago worms safely in suitable receptacles that have enough food and airflow for their voyage. Indicate the relevant details on the packaging, including the species name, amount, and provenance.

Collaborate with trustworthy shipping firms that have handled live animals for international shipping. For the worms to reach their destination securely and undamaged, make sure you follow their packaging and shipping instructions for live insects.

CHAPTER ELEVEN

RESOURCES FOR ADDITIONAL EDUCATION

SUGGESTED READINGS AND SOURCES

Getting access to the appropriate literature and materials is the first step toward becoming an expert in the field of edible sago worm cultivation. A great resource is "The Complete Guide to Edible Sago Worm Farming," an extensive handbook that addresses every aspect of saga worm farming, from initial setup to worm harvesting and processing. To ensure a thorough grasp of the procedure, this book not only offers step-by-step directions but also explores the science underlying the production of sago worms.

Online tools like blogs, articles, and websites devoted to sago worm farming can also be very helpful. Pages such as "SagoWormFarming101" include comprehensive instructions, troubleshooting advice, and case studies from seasoned farmers. These tools not only enhance your education but also offer real-world perspectives and workable answers to typical problems encountered by novices.

Examine scholarly publications and research papers about sago worm farming to expand your understanding. These academic materials explore cutting-edge methods, creative approaches, and the most recent advancements in the subject. By educating yourself on a variety of topics, you may create a solid foundation and keep up with how sago worm farming is changing.

FORUMS AND COMMUNITIES ONLINE

The vibrant online forums and communities devoted to sago worm farming are among the most helpful resources for novices in this field. Sites such as the "Sago Worm Farmers Network" and the "Sago Worm Enthusiasts Forum" unite farmers, specialists, and enthusiasts from all over the world, creating a cooperative learning and experience-sharing environment.

You can converse with other members of these communities, pose inquiries, and get guidance from seasoned farmers. To overcome obstacles and improve your agricultural techniques, community members' varied opinions and pooled knowledge might be rather helpful. Furthermore, these platforms frequently provide webinars, online workshops, and Q&A sessions, which offer continuing education possibilities.

Engaging in active participation in online groups and forums can help you advance your learning process by providing you with insightful knowledge and a supportive network. These online communities provide a plethora of tools and contacts to enhance your sago worm farming experience, whether you're looking for creative solutions, troubleshooting problems, or celebrating victories.

WORKSHOPS AND COURSES FOR TRAINING

Consider signing up for beginner-focused training workshops and courses if you want to learn sago worm farming through practical experience. Sustainable agriculture-focused institutions and groups frequently host seminars that address a range of worm farming topics, including sago worms. Typically, these courses blend didactic information with hands-on examples to provide attendees with direct experience.

Additionally, a structured curriculum covering everything from fundamental concepts to sophisticated procedures can be found in online courses taught by subject matter specialists. Websites such as "Sago Worm Farming Academy" provide video lessons, downloadable materials, and interactive modules aimed at meeting the needs of novices. You can gain confidence in your farming talents, study best practices, and develop critical skills by investing in formal training.

Additionally, completing certain seminars and courses can lead to accreditation, which can improve your reputation as a sago worm farmer. Regardless of your preference for online learning or in-person seminars, taking advantage of these educational options can quicken your learning curve and open doors to profitable farming endeavors.

EXPERT GUIDANCE & COACHING

Getting professional advice and mentorship is one of the best methods to accelerate your learning and success in sago worm farming. Based on their years of experience, seasoned farmers and business professionals can offer individualized counsel, customized recommendations, and practical insights. By interacting with mentors, you can benefit from their vast experience and steer clear of typical traps.

Look for mentors who are prepared to share their knowledge and techniques and who have a track record of success with sago worm farming. Making connections with seasoned professionals—whether through official mentorship programs or casual networking—can lead to beneficial opportunities and joint ventures. Regular check-ins, feedback meetings, and continuing support are common components of mentoring relationships, which guarantee continual development and progress.

Speaking with authorities in associated domains like sustainable agriculture, entomology, and business management can also help you make better decisions by expanding your viewpoint. By using the advice of mentors and advisors, you can improve your farming techniques, overcome obstacles more skillfully, and have long-term success with sago worm farming.

ONGOING EDUCATION IN THE PRODUCTION OF SAGO WORMS

Sago worm farming is an ongoing learning process that is characterized by skill development and education. Adopting an attitude of perpetual learning enables you to remain current with best practices, emerging technology, and industry trends. By investing time and energy into broadening your knowledge base, you'll be able to take advantage of new possibilities and adjust to changing problems.

Attend sago worm farming-related conferences, seminars, and industry events to participate in lifelong learning. These events offer chances for networking, access to state-of-the-art research, and perspectives from influential figures in the field. Engaging in panel discussions, workshops, and knowledge-sharing sessions enhances your comprehension and keeps you updated on developments in the field.

To expand your knowledge and competence in particular sago worm farming areas, you should also think about obtaining additional courses or certifications. Your farm's productivity and profitability can be increased with specialized training in areas like organic farming, value-added product development, and pest management. Adopting an attitude of lifelong learning will allow you to improve your abilities, innovate your methods, and prosper in the ever-changing world of sago worm farming.

www.ingramcontent.com/pod-product-compliance
Lightning Source LLC
Chambersburg PA
CBHW052335220526
45472CB00001B/435